THE
CONSUMER
UNDERGROUND

THE
CONSUMER
UNDERGROUND

BRILLIANT STRATEGIES FOR

CONSUMERS TO SAVE BIG

LIVING oUTSiDE THE
BoX

AN EXERCISE IN
CRITICAL THINKING

PAT PETERMAN

Table of Contents

Acknowledgments

This project was made possible by family and friends who over 20 years ago, encouraged me to capture "the process" in a usable format. Without such encouragement, I would have stalled the project for another 20 years...

...and still 20 more...

Introduction

Over 40 years ago I enlisted in the U. S. Marine Corps (devil-dog) to escape working in the bowels of a refinery in Detroit. I reasoned that death was a toss-up between the dangerous work and the homicidal co-workers. Two weeks into Marine Corps boot camp, I learned in a letter from my mother that the crew that I had worked with at the Detroit refinery murdered my boss. These junk yard dog – devil-dog roots motivated me to choose to become an advocate for my physical, emotional, and financial survival - first you must survive. So, over the decades I sought education, knowledge and self-improvement in these areas. Eventually I became pretty good at negotiating consumer outcomes and realized that I was following steps in a process that developed through failure and success. Following this process for the past few decades, I now presume successful outcomes. In the pages that follow, I share the recipe for this process with you. It's short with recurring doses of humor so you won't put the book down and then wait – let's say 20 years to finish it!

CHAPTER 1

BRILLIANT STRATEGIES FOR CONSUMERS TO SAVE BIG

Welcome to **THE CONSUMER UNDERGROUND**. This book is a how-to guide containing little known secrets to **save consumers thousands of $** per year. I will use various targeted strategies for reaching stress-free, positive outcomes.

I will include sample; **conversations, e-mails**, and **letters** that have been used successfully by the author. $ saving **solution strategies** will be featured in every chapter. These strategies have been developed from decades of field testing in the trenches of the American marketplace. There is no theory in this book. Best practices have evolved from lessons learned. The author has experienced a good dose of stress and conflict before discovering a repeatable strategy to avoid any stressful, unsuccessful outcomes.

Over time, I found that by implementing these strategies, I was able to avoid the conflict and financial risk/loss that is ever present in our consumer space. I will show you how to turn challenges into **opportunities to save you $**. I have had great (stress free) successes with these strategies for over 20 years now which has certainly spared me from a lot of frustration and saved me $.

Many of you have had successes resolving consumer challenges. For you - here is a **proven**, objective, repeatable process to expand your **solution tool box** for the future. For those readers who are seeking useful insight in such matters, this is your **startup plan** complete with step-by-step how-to instructions and examples. This book serves as a medium to share opportunities for success with you. Nothing in this book is represented as professional legal, insurance or financial advice. This is simply a collection of solution strategies to benefit consumers.

Together we will look at some common examples of **consumer challenges**. Then, we will solve each challenge by considering them as opportunities for stress-free, positive outcomes. We will also look at **smart retailing** strategies. Easy to use, **sample solution letters** are available in the Appendix for many common situations that you may encounter. You might find it useful to use these sample letters as a guide or template, modifying them with your specific information to fit your need.

For decades, the author has successfully practiced the strategies that I share in this book and (as I write this) am happily retired early in life looking from a mountain top at other snowcapped mountains.

Let's take a trip into **THE CONSUMER UNDERGROUND** with some proven strategies to get you to **your** mountain.

WHY DOES THIS MATTER?

The cost of a thing is the amount of what I call life which is required to be exchanged for it, immediately or in the long run.

Henry David Thoreau

The relationship between life and **work** and **debt** had to be different in the 1800s when Thoreau penned his quote didn't it? But Wait...

What do we **own** vs. what do we **owe**? Car...House...Bank Loans... - They own a piece of our life. The **car owns us!**

Where do we go to punch the "time clock"? - That company **owns a big piece of our life.**

The bank actually **owns "our" home** until the **final payment** is made - the Bank is our **landlord** until that day. But Wait... What? ...we thought we were homeowners!!! I guess that makes us just **mortgageowners!**

Damn! Thoreau was right!

Many if not most consumers choose to avoid; negotiating prices, returning items and pursuing product warranty claims, because we wish to avoid possible conflict. This results in our best interests not being fully represented. We accept undesirable outcomes. We try to forget about the **$ lost,** and to convince ourselves that it does not matter and is not worth the hassle and resulting stress.

Of course, there is the reality of the $ outcome, and knowing we have been **taken advantage of** is difficult to live with. Yet we avoid actively engaging a remedy to change the outcomes in our favor. We rationalize the **inaction** by convincing ourselves that our loss is the cost of doing business - caveat emptor.

Companies profit from consumers' **complacency**. After all, those company executives need someone to pay for the fuel for their private jets when they fly to the Bahamas and Aruba. Think about this first thing next Monday morning during the hours that you are on your company's clock **working** to **pay** for all those items that you paid full price for or those warranty and insurance claims that you did not fully pursue.

Listen . . . for the sound of that **corporate jet** flying south over your office building running on the fuel that **you helped pay for**!

Want to change this? Let's get off this **human hamster wheel**! Read on. **THE CONSUMER UNDERGROUND** has some answers!

CHAPTER 2

REAL WORLD EXAMPLES OF CONSUMER STRATEGIES:

1)   Roger red-tape a.k.a. I'm your friendly insurance agent until you file a claim:

Your insurance claim for hail or weather damage on your property was denied, yet your neighbor 's roof was replaced for $20,000.00 under their policy. (**how-to turn a few hours of your time into $38,000.00**)

2)   Carl the car gremlin:

The new automobile that you recently purchased has made far too many repair trips to the dealer 's service bay. (**the two hours spent on pursuing this opportunity nets you $1,027.00**)

3)   Internet retailer behemoth blues:

The merchandise that arrived very fast from your (and mine!) favorite on-line retailer (e-tailer) did not live up to your expectations and it's now past the warranty period. (**this strategy explains the secrets of e-tailing leverage**)

4)   Nancy no-can-do at the customer service/returns:

You walk into the mall/big box store with several bags of clothing or household items to be returned, only to be denied the return service due to various excuses: purchase was past 30 days, no original receipt, need to return directly to the manufacturer, owner/manager is not here today (likely vacationing in Hawaii), appears that you wore the item, no original tag on the item, or can 't find the item in their system. (**a proven, repeatable strategy to get past the human "firewall" of companies returns/customer service**)

5)   Terry teaser-rate:

The 6 months introductory rate on your smart phone service provider, satellite TV network, internet service provider, automobile satellite radio, or periodical subscriptions expire and the future rate is now 150% - 300% more $. (**this strategy can save us $100s per month**)

6)   New truck stops truckin:

Your 3 years old truck breaks down just 2 months after the new vehicle warranty expired, leaving you with a $5,473.43 tab. (**in this example, a few hours of our time saved us $5,473.43**)

7)   My car's replacement windshield isn't all it's cracked up to be:

Your insurance company assured you that the aftermarket replacement windshield they recommended was the equivalent of your Original Equipment Manufacturer (OEM) windshield. However, after replacement of the original damaged windshield, it now seems like you can hear more road noise. Also, the glass seems distorted near the edges and your Advanced Driver Assistance Systems (ADAS) are not working like they previously did! Does this aftermarket windshield offer the same structural rigidity for crash safety as the original? (**How to leverage the insurance company to replace our windshield with the proper OEM replacement part**)

Solution Strategy #1:

Opportunity:

Roger red-tape a.k.a. I'm your friendly insurance agent until you file a claim:

Your insurance claim for hail or weather damage on your property was denied, yet your neighbor's roof was replaced for $20,000.00 under their policy.

Solution:

This is a real-world example of a solution strategy that the author has personally used repeatedly with great success. In this example, we will not only be reimbursed to have our roof replaced for **$20,000.00**, but we will also discover damages and be reimbursed for an additional **$18,000.00**. Insurance companies don't want their policy holders knowing these secrets:

We have paid our insurance company in the past and still do to restore our potential losses in the future. Until we realize a loss, our insurance company's primary function is to collect $ from us. It is not until we incur a loss that we call upon these companies to perform the responsibilities for which we hired them in the first place. Therefore, it is quite reasonable to hold high expectations for their performance during the claim process.

The below example demonstrates a sample insurance solution strategy:

Is the claim fair and reasonable? We recall the weather event that caused the damage as significant. This is also evidenced by the damage of the neighbor's roof that was reimbursed for ($20,000.00) which is located only 28 feet from the edge of our roof. Now, let's look for potential points of leverage by exercising some diligence on the front end of the claim:

Gather information prior to the insurance representative's initial visit.

We found that 3 other neighbors on our block will be reimbursed by their insurance companies for their roof damage.

We found archived weather data specific to location and date to include satellite imagery. We make copies to have available to present to the insurance representative.

We took pictures of the weather event, hail, and damaged areas during and immediately after the event.

Review insurance policy.

Review industry criteria for establishing similar claims (e. g. % of granular loss and size of hail dimples on shingles, etc.).

We cold-call roofing companies and talked with Harold Helpful at ACME roofing who was very friendly and informative about industry standards for claims. He provides us with a few tips on what to tell the insurance representative to enhance our chance of achieving a successful claim. We might even have Harold come over prior to our insurance representative's visit to assess the roof damage for us and give us a ballpark cost of repair/replacement. Harold was very helpful because he was interested in getting the first opportunity at the roof replacement project estimate. After we successfully settle the claim with our insurance company, we offer Harold the first opportunity to bid on the roof replacement.

We also look at areas of our property for weather/hail loss and not focus just on the roof. Because we "look/live outside the box" we expand our focus on the scope of loss and inspect property such as: gutters, siding, window sills, patio, furniture, fence, flower pots, outdoor decorations, etc.

This research is worth our time because of the potential value of the claim ($20,000.00).

Because of the couple of hours spent on the above information gathering, we have many points of leverage identified. We are ready to meet with the insurance representative.

We make the time to meet with the insurance representative (or their subcontractor) when they arrive to evaluate our claim. We will be the most polite, friendly, and non-threatening customer that this representative has dealt with this week. We are also well informed due to the research that we conducted. We know that the remedy we are seeking (the insurance claim) is fair and reasonable because we have assessed the damage and know the replacement/repair costs.

Roger Red-tape arrives at our house and we present the above information that we gathered prior to his visit. We are in fact, very well prepared which boosts our confidence. We are in control of this process and will lead Roger through areas/items that we need to be addressed and offer supporting information that we previously gathered as needed. Our insurance company's best interest is in doing the right thing for us and we are facilitating this process to ensure that they align with our desired remedy. We take notes during this visit.

Due to our diligent information gathering, and thinking/living outside-the box, we discovered damaged areas outside the usual scope of loss (roof) for weather/hail events. Roger Red-tape now becomes Roger Remedy. Roger approves the claim for damaged: roof, fence, flower pots, patio table, chairs, deck finish, window sills, siding, and gutters. Roger writes us a check for **$38,000.00**.

Using this strategy, we were not only successful in having our roof replaced for **$20,000.00**, but we also discovered damages that were reimbursed for an additional **$18,000.00**. This additional damage might not have otherwise been discovered.

Appendix A contains sample correspondence which you can use as an example that you would send to the insurance representative to summarize the inspection and promised resolution. The solution example of this insurance claim can be repeated for other type of claims (flood, lightning, tornado, hurricane, fire, etc.) by substituting claim-specific information.

If we don't reach a remedy with the insurance representative, then we have the option of going to Chapter 6 to implement a detailed process. This process takes a little more time, and it is often the best path for resolution on these higher $ remedies.

Solution Strategy #2:

Opportunity:

Carl the car gremlin:

The new automobile that you recently purchased has made far too many repair trips to the dealer's service bay.

Solution:

This is another real-world example of a solution strategy that the author has personally used repeatedly with great success. Many consumers do not understand that they might have a point of leverage with automobile manufacturers. (The two hours spent on pursuing this opportunity is $1,027.00).

The below example demonstrates a sample automobile reliability issue solution strategy:

> Last May, I purchased a new ACME Silver Express Minivan for $42,460.00. I was excited to experience the reliability and luxury of a new car. Unfortunately, the promise of excellence of ACME Automobile Inc. has not been a reality for me and my family.
>
> After I purchased my ACME Silver Express Minivan last May, I experienced four failures of electrical control systems. These electric failures have had a negative impact on me and my family.

It is fair and reasonable that we seek resolution from the automobile manufacturer for the above situation? We are not going to negotiate with the automotive **dealership** or their service department because we know that we have no point of leverage with them, so we would be wasting our time. But Wait... The automobile **manufacturer** might be a great point of leverage!

The automobile manufacturer represents the product (minivan). It is this product that is at issue, not the service to try to remedy the issue with the product. Our point of leverage is that we spent over forty-two thousand dollars with the expectation of quality and reliability that was represented by ACME. ACME is motivated to maintain high customer feedback ratings and positive public relations, product referrals, and repeat sales.

Spend a few minutes on an internet search to see if there is a recurring issue with ACME Express Minivan electrical control system failures. If not, this is no problem. If yes, this becomes an additional point of leverage as the manufacturer likely is aware of this defect with their ACME Express Minivan.

Conduct an internet search to locate the contact information for ACME Automobile Inc. customer relations division. Call this (automobile manufacturer) contact and be the most polite, courteous, and patient customer that they have dealt with this month. Next, provide them a very brief overview of the situation. Ask if they are the person that can assist you with fair consideration for your situation. If not, ask that they connect you with that person.

Next, provide the more detailed history of the situation such as described in this example:

> The first electrical control system failure was on June 9, 2018. I was without the vehicle for 3 days and had to take time off work and drive the vehicle in for service and pick it up after the service was completed.

> The second electrical control system failure was on September 21, 2018. I was without the vehicle for 5 days and had to take time off work and drive the vehicle in for service and pick it up after the service was completed. I also

paid out of pocket $342.00 for a rental car for this time frame.

The third electrical control system failure was On October 14, 2019. I was without the vehicle for 2 days and had to take time off work and drive the vehicle in for service and pick it up after the service was completed.

The fourth electrical control system failure was on November 9, 2019. I was without the vehicle for 3 days and had to take time off work and drive the vehicle in for service and pick it up after the service was completed.

The service advisor stated she was not confident that they have the recurring electrical failure figured out. This is a recurring problem and I have little confidence in the reliability of my ACME Silver Express Minivan.

Next, you describe the negative impact on your time. Your time = financial impact:

I understand that these issues have been repaired as covered by my warranty. This is not the issue. Because of the above mechanical failures, I had to take off many hours from my work (unpaid time off) that I will not be reimbursed for. Many hours were also spent communicating with the service advisor to coordinate the repairs and scheduling of the automobile transportation to and from the dealership service center. I asked several friends for favors driving me to the dealership.

I am not seeking to gain financially, only to be provided consideration for the negative impact that this has caused me.

In consideration of the above facts, you ask ACME Automobile Inc. to provide consideration for the inconveniences and lost time at work that was incurred. You mention that in situations such as this, you understand that sometimes ACME Automotive compensates customers for their next month **$685.00** car payment and reimbursement for the **$342.00** car rental.

Is this something that you can approve, or do you need your supervisor's approval

Again, I am not seeking to gain financially, only to be provided consideration for the negative impact that this has caused me. Is the consideration I just described something that you have the authority to approve? If not, please connect me with the person that does.

Would you like me to send you a receipt for the $342.00 car rental and my car payment information?

Yes, I understand that you need management approval for this before you can commit to anything. I have already spent too much time with these issues with my minivan and wish to put this issue behind me. Is November 24 enough time for you to provide me with a response? May I please have the spelling of your last name and your position with ACME?

Appendix B contains sample correspondence which you can use as an example that you would send the automobile manufacturers representative to summarize the situation and/or reiterate the promised resolution.

Solution Strategy #3:

Opportunity:

Internet retailer behemoth blues:

The merchandise that arrived very fast from your (and mine!) favorite on-line retailer (e-tailer) did not live up to your expectations and it's now past the warranty period.

Solution:

Consumers are experiencing the many **benefits of scale** when retailing with the **giant internet platforms**. Some of the benefits are: fast and cheap/free shipping terms, expansive product selection, ease of purchase transactions, search engines for comparing, sorting and selecting products, lower prices, data streaming services, and consumer reviews of products via reputational feedback systems.

For the purpose of our solution strategy, the benefit of third-party seller reputational feedback provides a tremendous point of leverage for the buyer. These third-party sellers (also known as "the seller") partner to sell their products with giant on-line retailers. They are usually very motivated to work with the buyer to make sure that they receive positive feedback responses from the buyer. Such positive responses are valued by the seller because of potential increased future sales, and to maintain in good standing with the on-line retail platform.

We are going to send the seller an e-mail to request a remedy. This is where our point of leverage is - with the seller. Communicating with the giant internet platform is not the best option at this point. The platform relies on the various (third party) sellers that they partner with to resolve such issues. These sellers usually do not offer much phone service so e-mailing is usually an effective means of communicating with these companies.

Often the seller will e-mail you after the initial purchase to establish communication. You can also find the sellers e-mail from the on-line retailer's website. We start with this seller's e-mail contact.

For this example, the product had a 30-day warranty. These solar powered lights worked great for a few months but quit working after that. This is not consistent with the positive reviews of the product and we had higher expectations. We aren't going to discuss the 30-day warranty in this e-mail because we consider the warranty as just a guideline to keep the majority of customers from pursuing a remedy. The reality is that the warranty is binding and we most likely have no formal, legal recourse, but we are simply asking for a remedy based on the good faith of the seller. We think this is a fair and reasonable remedy to ask for.

If the seller rejects our request, we have only spent 5 stress-free minutes writing a simple e-mail pursuing the solution. If this request comes back with a negative reply, we are going to drop it. No worries, in the author's experience, the sellers in these situations are eager to do the right thing if it is fair and reasonable. Just remember that your success rate with this strategy will diminish with higher priced products due to the financial impact on the seller.

We will be the most polite, friendly, and non-threatening customer that this seller's customer service representative has dealt with today. It is the appropriate way to treat people and will give us our best opportunity for favorable resolution. A detailed email example is available in Appendix C. Here is a quick example of the e-mail:

> To: (retrieve the seller's previous e-mail that you received when you purchased the item and reply to their e-mail)
>
> Subject: (enter the seller's item # and order # here followed by re- your last name)

Dear ACME Solar Light company,

I was excited to purchase and receive my solar powered outside lights #xxxx that I ordered from you on xxxx. Based on the numerous positive reviews of these lights, your company's upstanding reputation, and after reading your product description, I was sure that these lights would be a perfect solution for my outside porch lighting needs.

After I first installed the lights, I was impressed with the amount of light and how long the batteries held a charge - just like in the reviews! Unfortunately, after a few months, the lights stopped working. I am disappointed that the lights failed to work as represented and am contacting you about replacing them with units that work as advertised.

I look forward to receiving the replacement units so that I can enjoy the same positive experience as thousands of your other customers. I look forward to providing prompt positive feedback regarding this issue.

Sincerely

Pat, address, phone#

The next day or two, we receive a letter notifying that the seller is sending replacement lights at no charge. Often, the seller won't even request us to return the defective product. We will certainly take the time to provide this seller positive feedback as they certainly deserve it!

A stress-free win-win!

Solution Strategy #4:

Opportunity:

Nancy no-can-do at the customer service/returns:

You walk into the mall/big box store with several bags of clothing or household items to be returned, only to be denied the return service due to various excuses: purchase was past 30 days, no original receipt, need to return directly to the manufacturer, owner/manager is not here today (likely vacationing in Aruba), appears that you wore the item, no original tag on the item, or can't find the item in their system.

Solution:

In this opportunity, customer satisfaction feedback is the primary point of leverage. Another point of leverage is that some/many customer service representatives truly want to help people out.

We were going back to the big box store or retail clothing chain for a future purchase, so bringing the items that we intend to return is no burden. The remedy that we will be seeking is fair and reasonable when seeking this resolution. Once again, we are going to be the most polite, friendly, and non-threatening customer that this retailer's customer service representative has dealt with today. This is how we want to be treated, and what a great way to treat other people. We start the conversation by asking how their day is going, how they are doing.

We are not going to inquire about return policies - why arm them with a justification for denying us the return? We start with asking the representative whether the refund will be applied back on our credit card, or will we get cash back (implying that we will be successful in the return, and we know what we are doing). Be confident and you will likely control this outcome. We will attempt to resolve most returns with this first line representative. But for those few instances when we run into Robert a.k.a. Bob by-the-book, lets continue.

Returns clerk; "Sir, you don't have a receipt and I can't find a history of purchase at this store for these items." We help them find the pathway to our desired remedy. In this situation, we ask them to scan the tag on the garment, or the box that the $500.00 vacuum cleaner came in for the identification and price. And we are o.k. with a store credit for these items with no sales receipt. Maintain your confidence and don't be demanding or rude.

If we don't reach resolution with this representative, we can ask for the supervisor and repeat the above approach with the supervisor. We communicate to the supervisor that this isn't the customer service that we expected from this store. "And no, we were not aware of the store policy that vacuum cleaners could not be returned." This policy was never communicated to us before we made the purchase. If we were aware of such policy, we certainly would not have purchased the $500.00 vacuum."

We ask the supervisor if they can resolve this today. If not, (considering it was a $500.00 purchase), and we are already in the store, it's worth our time to attempt to reach resolution with the store manager. If we dead-end with the store manager, we wish them a good day and politely ask for the correct spelling of their last name.

For those readers who are not successful with this initial strategy and wish to pursue this further to resolution: We have the option of going to Chapter 6 to implement a detailed process. An e-mail/letter example is provided in Appendix D for a sample to use for this solution. The detailed process takes a little more time and it is often the best path for resolution on higher $ remedies.

Solution Strategy #5:

Opportunity:

Terry teaser-rate:

The 6 months introductory rate on your smart phone service provider, satellite TV network, internet service provider, automobile satellite radio, or periodical subscriptions expired and the future rate is now 150% - 300% more $.

Solution:

Re-negotiate recurring $ contracts:

Call your: satellite, cable, phone, and internet service providers and request a discounted monthly rate. Be polite, friendly, and confident. Ask what current discount packages are available. Inquire about a loyalty discount.

If the service representative (or their supervisor) cannot grant you the discount that you are requesting, ask to be transferred to the department or a person who is authorized to provide you the discount. Often you will end up at the customer loyalty or customer retention department or a similar department where customers are routed to offer discounts to keep customers from switching to another service provider. This is the department where you will have the best leverage.

Keep track of when your preferred (teaser) rate expires on subscriptions such as satellite radio, periodicals (print and digital), etc. This is important, as some of these rates will automatically increase up to 400% without notification after the preferred rate expires.

A few days prior to the expiration of the preferred rate, call the company and request that the preferred rate be extended. If you remain confident and steadfast with your request, you will often be granted a discounted rate.

Don't underestimate the importance of confidence and composure in these negotiations. The representatives that you are dealing with are not used to customers being in control of themselves, let alone the discussion.

Also, realize that we will not always be successful requesting the above discounts. Some companies do have firm fixed pricing structures, but not most.

Solution Strategy #6:

Opportunity:

New truck stops truckin:

Your 3 years old truck breaks down just 2 months after the new vehicle warranty expired, leaving you with a $5,473.43 tab.

Solution:

Since automobile maintenance and warranty issues are major expenses in most budgets, we will look at another solution strategy on automobiles - this time on warranty issues. (**In this example, a few hours of our time saved us $5,473.43**).

This is yet another example of a solution strategy that the author has personally used numerous times with great success. We are going to pursue a point of leverage with the automobile manufacturer:

> We purchased our 2016 ACME 4x4 Triplecab truck in
> February of 2016. We had great previous experience with
> ACME trucks and therefore developed high expectations
> for their reliability. This was a primary consideration in the

purchase decision. We have had required service performed at ACME Automotive Big Johnson's Dealership. We also had several oil changes performed at the local spiffy-chimp lube. We have all the receipts to prove that we have kept up with the required manufacturer's maintenance schedule.

Understand that this is an out of warranty request for consideration and that you have no recourse other than to appeal to the good faith of the automobile manufacturer's integrity. The truck was only 2 months out of warranty coverage and had far less mileage that the warranty allowed. We are still out of warranty because the terms are months/mileage, whichever occurs first. Is it fair and reasonable that we pursue consideration from the automobile manufacturer for the above situation? We are not going to pursue consideration from the automotive dealership or their service department, we will deal directly with the automobile manufacturer.

Our point of leverage is that we spent over forty-six thousand dollars with the expectation of quality and reliability that was represented by ACME. ACME is motivated to maintain high customer feedback ratings and positive public relations - excellence and integrity. Spend a few minutes on an internet search to see if there is a recurring issue with ACME truck transmission and air conditioning failures. If not, this is no problem, if yes, this becomes an additional point of leverage as the manufacturer likely is aware of this defect with their ACME trucks.

We are going to initiate contact a customer service representative at the automobile manufacturer - ACME. Conduct an internet search to locate the contact information for ACME Automotive Inc. customer relations division. We call the contact and are the most polite, courteous, confident and patient customer that they have dealt with this month. Remember we are seeking only to be reimbursed for repairs on the vehicle that ACME manufactured with the expectation of excellent reliability. We share that expectation of excellence with the manufacturer. Provide the initial ACME representative with a very brief overview of the situation. Ask this representative if they are the person that can assist you with fair consideration for your situation. If not, ask that they connect you with that person, and then provide a detailed timeline and narrative outlining the problems that we had with our vehicle.

Here is an example:

> On April 5, 2019, at only 24,408 miles, my ACME 4x4 Triplecab was repaired for an air conditioning manifold leak, which resulted in total charges of $1,193.43 and a second trip to ACME Automotive Big Johnson's Dealership (and another five mile bike ride from home) to have it re-fixed (during the first repair, the equipment at Big Johnson's overcharged the a/c system).

> On April 15, at only 25,221 miles, my ACME Triplecab was repaired for a transmission replacement. After discussions with ACME Automotive Customer Service Division, (and

after initially being told repeatedly that there was nothing that they could do for me), I ended up paying $4,280.00 to have the transmission with only 25,221 miles replaced with a new one.

Now, let's talk about how the truck failed our **expectations of excellence** as represented by the manufacturer:

My expectations for the ACME 4x4 Triplecab truck were that I would realize more than 24,408 miles of air conditioning utility prior to the failure of this system. My expectations were that I would realize more than 25,221 miles of transmission utility prior to the total failure of the transmission. These failures happened only 2 months after the expiration of my new vehicle's 3 years, 40,000 miles warranty.

I would like to believe my experience is the exception. I trust that you will preserve the **credibility and integrity** of ACME Automotive Inc. and stand behind the unfortunate mechanical and service failures that I have experienced. To accomplish this, I believe it fair for ACME Automotive to reimburse me for the above repair costs. I feel that my expectations for reliability have been reasonable. I would like to once again purchase and recommend your products.

If you feel however, that my expectations for reliability for my 2016 ACME 4x4 Triplecab truck have been unreasonable, and that the above failures should be expected from ACME products - **just two months out of the warranty period**, with much less mileage than allotted during the warranty period, than please let me know this!

Next, we assist the customer service representative with their company's goal of customer satisfaction:

Is this something that you can approve, or do you need your supervisor's approval?

Again, we are only seeking to be reimbursed for repairs on the vehicle. Is the consideration I just described something that you have the authority to act on? If not, please inform me who that person is. Would you like me to send you a receipt for the $5,473.43 that I paid for the air conditioning and transmission repair/replacement?

This person might be motivated to help you but may need final approval from their boss. This is acceptable so let's pin them down on a date for this:

Yes, I understand that you need management approval for this before you commit to reimbursing me for the $5,473.43. I have already spent too much time with these issues with my truck and wish to put all of this behind me.

Is April 24 enough time for you to provide me with a response? May I please have the spelling of your last name and your position with ACME?

Appendix E contains sample correspondence which you can use as an example that you would send the automobile manufacturer's representative to summarize the situation or reiterate the promised resolution.

Solution Strategy #7:

Opportunity:

My car's replacement windshield isn't all it's cracked up to be:

Your insurance company assured you that the aftermarket replacement windshield they recommended was the equivalent of your Original Equipment Manufacturer (OEM) windshield. However, after replacement of the original damaged windshield, it now seems like you can hear more road noise. Also, the glass seems distorted near the edges and your Advanced Driver Assistance Systems (ADAS) are not working like they previously did! Does this aftermarket windshield offer the same structural rigidity for crash safety integrity as the original?

Solution:

The author was a slow learner with this one. It took bad experiences with several non-OEM aftermarket windshield replacements that "met or exceeded DOT minimum safety standards" to learn the lesson.

The standard routine - We call the insurance company to report a cracked windshield claim. The insurance company states that they use an aftermarket glass company that is affiliated with the insurance company. Next, we are assured that this aftermarket windshield will meet or exceed minimum DOT standards and is as good as the original that came with our car. The insurance company has partnered this windshield company for years and can schedule a prompt appointment to take care of the replacement at our location. The insurance representative does not even bring up the OEM replacement option, saving the insurance company hundreds of dollars per claim by steering the uninformed customer into the cheaper glass. But wait, I want the safe (more expensive) OEM good-stuff damnit!

DOT - Department of Transportation minimum standards automobile glass standard is not a baseline for excellence! Automobile manufacturers routinely use glass that has superior; fit, finish, optical accuracy and safety than aftermarket windshields. This results in automobile replacement glass that can cost substantially more than aftermarket replacement glass. Advanced Driver Assistance Systems such as: adaptive cruise control, glare-free high beam, pixel light, adaptive light control, automatic parking, collision mitigation braking system, blind spot monitor, automatic night vision, navigation system, forward collision warning, radar, camera, lane departure warning, advanced driver assistance system, etc. all require ocular clarity and accuracy. The windshield is designed and manufactured to integrate with these advanced vehicle technologies. Aftermarket glass does not always account for these complex electrical components and may interfere with your vehicle's electronic safety systems or cause them to not function properly. Do you wish to chance potential failures with any of these safety systems that are dependent on OEM glass to function reliably?

Also, automotive glass is important for vehicle safety structural rigidity for crashworthiness.

There is a common thread running through this narrative - **safety, safety, and more safety**, now we have a point of **leverage**.

First, take the time to read your automobile insurance policy regarding comprehensive coverage on your vehicle. Next, we contact the insurance company representative to report the initial claim and request OEM replacement glass. Be prepared for the sales pitch from the insurance representative about how great that the aftermarket windshield is and how this is what all policyholders routinely have used for 20 years. Then, we ask this representative if there is an additional cost to us for the OEM glass. If the OEM glass is the same cost to us as the aftermarket glass, I'm going with the good stuff that came on my car. If there is an additional cost to us for the OEM, then we may have to consider paying out of pocket for the upgrade.

But Wait! don't pay out of pocket yet, the OEM replacement option might be necessary to ensure the safety of the vehicle's integrated systems which include the windshield and all other glass in the vehicle.

Contact the automobile manufacturer and inquire as to what they recommend for replacement glass. The manufacturer's position on this matter may even presently exist in writing on their website or elsewhere online. The author recently completed research on this and found that many automobile manufacturer's now have written positions that recommend OEM replacement for all glass for structural integrity safety and (ADAS) systems safety reasons.

Once we have our car manufacturer's position on this matter, we contact the insurance company to inform them of our car manufacturer's important safety recommendations for OEM glass replacement. We make sure that they get our e-mail stating the car manufacturer's position on this subject and that the e-mail highlights the numerous safety considerations. If the insurance company still refuses to replace our windshield with the safe OEM glass at no additional cost to you then tell the representative you want this denial of manufacturer's recommended safe glass replacement in writing. It is doubtful that an insurance company will state in writing that they denied you a safe windshield replacement.

Appendix F contains sample correspondence which you can use as an example that you would send the insurance representative to inform them of the car manufacturer's position on this matter. In the sample letter, we include the manufacturer's important recommendation for OEM glass replacement due to numerous safety considerations.

CHAPTER 3

THE SHEEPING OF CONSUMERS - SMART RETAILING
STRATEGIES

So long as they (the Proles) continued to work and breed, their other activities were without importance. Left to themselves, like cattle turned loose upon the plains of Argentina, they had reverted to a style of life that appeared to be natural to them, a sort of ancestral pattern...Heavy physical work, the care of home and children, petty quarrels with neighbors, films, football, beer and above all, gambling filled up the horizon of their minds. To keep them in control was not difficult.

George Orwell

Incredibly, Orwell penned this quote in the year 1948. Has human/consumer **behavior** changed since then?

As modern-day consumers, we have been **conditioned** to accept many of the following as normal conditions of doing business:

- Long lines for extended periods of time
- Products that target our need to participate in the latest must-have high-cost fad
- Rude and non-accommodating customer service and returns departments where you are treated as the "defendant"
- Automobile service departments that have a different (read-more frequent) maintenance schedule than the automobile manufacturer to enhance their profit at your expense
- Separate, less favorable pricing structure for consumers who do not negotiate for the lower prices
- Insurance companies who issue lower claim payouts to less informed customers
- Warranty terms that often expire shortly before the item fails
- Normalizing debt (e.g. the average car loan is now approximately five-and-a-half years with 8-year loans available)

We cannot control these conditions however we can exercise control over how they impact us - emotionally and $. The next few sections will challenge convention, and we will continue to use examples of real-world how-to solutions here at **THE CONSUMER UNDERGROUND**!

SMART RETAILING STRATEGIES: (maximizing your purchasing $ through savvy spending)

The net effect of paying more than we should is that it keeps us in the workplace - **human habitrail** longer than we would otherwise be if we kept more of our $. We call it **TGIF** and not **TGIM** for a reason! If we have already exited the **human habitrail**, then the result is less $ available to spend in retirement.

Let's look at some **strategies** to **change this**!

Shop for deeply discounted merchandise:

Thrift shop in certain demographics and we can find the **buys of a lifetime**! $400 Nordic sweaters with the tags on for $20, vintage sporting goods and collectibles, unused $300.00 designer purses for $15.00 etc. Thrift stores provide an opportunity for **one-of-a-kind** items at **once-in-a-lifetime discounts**.

We feel great about donating items to charities like Goodwill, but it is not until those items are sold that these organizations benefit. You are donating to these charities when you purchase their goods and you can also feel great about that terrific deal that your discovered!

On-line discount retailers seem to offer better deals every year. New name brand, high end, discontinued and overstocked merchandise can be found for up to **95% off**. Do a quick internet search for the category that you are interested in and take it from there. Bikes and bike gear, snowshoes, backpacks, fly rods, yoga clothing, footwear, camping gear, jackets, paddle boarding gear, etc. We see this stuff offered year-round for 40%-95% off.

Ask for discounts:

We ask for a discount every time we take the car in for service. Do this in person when talking with the service advisor: "Jim, will you apply the coupon that the company has been mailing out like Janet did for me last time I was here?" Or: "I bought my car and truck here will you guys still give me the **10% loyalty** discount that I **always** get?"

Requesting a discount when calling to make the appointment is a good bet, but with auto service in such demand, this leverage is not what it used to be. A quick internet search for discount coupons is a better use of time on the front end. We will also ask the auto dealer or independent service store to honor competitors' discount offers. Same strategy for the automotive lubrication chains. Using these strategies, the author hasn't paid full price for an oil change at the **spiffy-chimp lube** stores for decades.

Most retail stores in the USA obviously have firm, fixed pricing structures and such prices are usually displayed for each item, but clothing retailers and big box stores often offer **discounts** that are not **advertised**. Day of the week discounts, military discounts, senior discounts, AARP member discounts, AAA discounts, and other membership considerations are often worth asking for. At checkout, ask for the **discount coupon(s)** that were sent out in the store's recent mailer to be applied.

Requesting a discount from a **construction/remodel contractor** is a mixed bag. Market conditions - demand of the craft are important considerations when considering this.

Rental car companies are an example of how to pursue several **discount strategies** on one purchase:

Choose your location (market) and dates and conduct a **quick internet price comparison** for a couple rental companies. Next, the author always calls to personally work with the representative.

We will be the **friendliest** and most considerate customer that this representative has dealt with in a long time. This is not difficult because many customers are rude and patronizing towards the representative. But we are kindly asking for consideration. Wouldn't you grant the most favorable **discount to your friend?** We consider the **advertised rates** as "teaser" rates and will ask the representative for final pricing including tax (if not, you cannot accurately compare pricing between companies).

First, we ask for **specials** or discounts that are not listed or advertised. Good, got the special, this is a good **starting point**. But Wait! we still want **more discounts**, so we inquire as to what other discount consideration would be best; AARP, Military, my company, my car insurance company, my credit card company, etc.

We are not finished asking for discounts, so we ask the representative if they have a **"coupon"** that they can apply. Finally, if we are not at the rate that we intended to end up at, we ask for a price **match on an advertised** rate that a **competitor** rental car company is offering.

Beware of additional charges that you may not need such as insurance on the rental car. Check first with your insurance company to see if they cover your rental.

When we end up with a great price, we make sure to complete the customer survey after the transaction as the representative deserves the positive feedback.

The **ten minutes** that you spent on this transaction could save you **$150.00** on a one-week rental which equates to you being paid the equivalent of **$900.00 per hour** for your time spent on this! Use this same example strategy for negotiating discounts on other products or services.

Research big-ticket items:

A good practice is to **reserve spending more time** on researching for **higher priced goods or services**. One caveat is that all items where **safety** is important require thorough research - first you must survive!

Car purchases/leases and car maintenance are perhaps the second biggest ticket item purchases that we make second only to our homes. Let's look at automobile purchasing/leasing. Quite frankly, the author starts with the safety/crash test data and proceeds from there. Automobiles that fail the National Highway Traffic Safety Administration (NHTSA) crash tests are still allowed to be sold and driven on America's roads! Do you want to be driving in one of these (millions sold) automobiles that fail the crash testing protocol? Resources such as: Consumer Reports, Edmunds.com, nhtsa.gov, and iihs.org, J. D. Powers are just a few examples of references available for automobile reliability, safety, and owner satisfaction. Credit unions, membership retail stores, buying representatives, rental companies, wholesalers, on-line companies (Autotrader, Craigslist, etc.) are among options for purchasing automobiles. Price shopping has never been more transparent. Most dealerships use aggressive on-line pricing of current inventory which sometimes represents their lowest pricing.

When selling a used vehicle, beware of fraudulent forms of payment such as: bank checks, cashier's checks, personal checks, money orders, counterfeit currency, etc. Your bank or credit union could be a good resource for advice on such transactions.

When researching automobile tire purchase decisions, the author starts with resources such as tirerack.com tire surveys which provides feedback from users on various tire brands. Next, I do comparison shopping for tires and consider price, service and location as major factors in choosing tire stores.

Location - We are not benefiting by driving **40 miles** vs. 5 miles to the tire store **every 5,000 miles** to have our tires rotated just to save $100 on the price of the tires. Remember, that's 9 times you will take the **80-mile round trip for a 50,000 miles rated tire life**. Always consider the bigger picture and the long term.

Verify discounts/sale prices (at checkout) on items that you purchase:

A few years ago, most grocery (and some other retail) stores adopted software that delays the credit for all discounted items until the **end of the total sale**. This strategy, along with **moving the checkout screen(s) farther** away from the customer, make it difficult to **verify that you are correctly charged** for the goods which you are paying for. The other day, while shopping with my partner at the local organic triple natural healthy products grocery store, the author sought out to prove the theory that many sale items are **not correctly priced at the check-out register**. I bet my partner that some discounted items would not ring up correctly. Waiting until all the items were entered into the checkout computer, I politely asked the clerk to check to see if the discounted items were rung up appropriately. After some minutes of the clerk performing some computer alchemy and then looking at the results on the screen, it was confirmed that no sale items were correctly priced at the checkout. I took the clerk's word for this (as they appropriately adjusted the prices) because I couldn't see the small screen located some six feet away. I hate to win bets like this! It is rare when I observe a customer questioning such things. What if they had charged me $60.00 for the gluten-free non-GMO Japanese parsnip and I failed to verify the price charged?

One well-known national clothing chain where the author frequently shopped (for years) applied an **incorrect discount 100% of the time**! I believe that was intentional, and I never observed one customer checking the math at the checkout register or otherwise verifying that the correct discount was applied. The discounts on the garment tags were always **coded incorrectly**, (in the store's favor of course) so I had to walk their employees through the math during the checkout process. I continued shopping there only because they offered up to **85% discounts** and I always ended up adjusting the price correctly at the checkout.

I don't see consumers working a calculator at the register to ensure that the sale price rang up correctly. Use your calculator, items are regularly coded incorrectly! Take out your smart phone calculator at the register and verify the correct discount: Let's look at the example of 70% off $100.00. 70% off 100% original price = 30% of original price. 30% = .3 x original price of $100.00 is $30.00. Do this quick math at the register.

Perform this easy calculation at the register, you are standing there waiting anyway!

Make receipt files:

Keep receipts and **warranty information** from items that you purchase. Make a habit of placing these **records in labeled files** when you return home.

With a physical store receipt (or retrieved from e-mail receipt file) you have **more leverage when you return items**.

In the event of **theft, flood, fire,** or other insurance loss, the receipts may prove value of the loss.

For **warranty claims,** you will have copies of the terms of such coverage to refer to during a warranty claim.

Seasonal Timing:

Time your clothing shopping to take advantage of end of season **clearances.**

Big box stores also often **discount merchandise aggressively** if they fail to **liquidate** in their previous end of **season sales,** A seasonal item that was stored in the back of the warehouse all winter is now an outdated model that does not make sense in their current spring inventory. An example of this strategy is that recently, the author held out purchasing a new mulching lawnmower that I wanted and needed. By waiting through the fall sales, and through the winter into early spring, my patience was rewarded as I purchased the **$196.00** lawnmower for **$80.00.**

Stores who have price/coupon matching guarantees are a plus:

Many stores match sales prices of their competitors. This offers us an opportunity to conduct business at our **preferred store** (near us with the good service). We shop at our favorite store and obtain the **discount prices** of the discount store in the undesirable part of town with the poor service.

CHAPTER 4

THINK OUTSIDE THE MATRIX (BOX) - WHAT BOX? (a.k.a. living outside the box)

If you would be a real seeker of truth, it is necessary at least once in your life you doubt, as far as possible, all things.

Rene Descartes (circa 1637)

The **box of convention.** Since birth, we are **socially engineered** to believe that there are **boundaries** and **parameters** defining **limits** on the scope of our potential **thoughts and actions.** We eschew the laws of quantum theory. We are marketed to mold our minds, bodies, actions, and thoughts to live in the **matrix "box" of society.** We are taught what "**normal**" should look like, and how much it **should cost.** Many in society subscribe to this **narrative fallacy of conformity.** This effectively creates **prodigious populations** of **voracious consumers.** We purchase things that we **really don't need** so that we feel like we **fit in** with others who are purchasing things that they don't need to be like us. We **incur debt** doing this and we work extra hours, weeks, months and years to pay the **price of fitting in.**

When we have reached adult age, we are instructed that we are allowed to "**think outside the box**"...Wow!,..woohoo! let me get out, stretch my legs, get some fresh air, and engage in 5 minutes of free/**critical thinking**, thank you so much!

Box? What box? There never was a box, it does not exist.

We defined the norms and imposed boundaries on ourselves. As a consumer, that's why we stand in line to pay full price for something so we can feel like we fit in with all the other people living in the box. We avoid **challenging convention** because of the potential negative stress.

Let's look at one example of how we are **socially engineered**: - **Life Insurance**: Flood insurance pays for flood damage, fire insurance pays in the event of a fire, theft insurance pays in the event of a theft. Than what is life insurance? There is no policy for us that is redeemable if we in fact live! So... **Life Insurance must really be Death Insurance** since it pays upon our death! Life insurance should mean; maintaining your health, accident avoidance, safely driving a large safe automobile, personal defense, saving money through **THE CONSUMER UNDEGROUND** Smart Consumer Strategies so that you can **retire early** and not die from working forever, etc.

Now, we are going to **leave this box** and **think for ourselves**.

A look at life outside the box - lets engage **critical thinking**, and rational thinking. Question our **emotions and assumptions** when we represent our consumer interests. These are, in fact **business transactions**! Critical thinking is **antithetical to herd mentality, conformity**. Ego and emotion are what differentiates the herd from the critical thinker who understands that **confident objectivity is a subtle yet powerful virtue.**

An example of **critical thinking**. Trash Collectors, Customer Service Clerks, Physicians, Dentists, Government Officials - they all **work for us**. Their job is to assist us in meeting our needs and their goal is getting paid for providing customer satisfaction. I task them equally according to my need, not according to their title, rank or their standing in the food chain hierarchy. Respectful always to the person but, if I engage in any ass-kissing, it will be with the lowest ranking, least paid. A famous author once stated that he judges people by how well they treat the lowest paid person that they meet that day. This is a good rule to live by and is officially adopted as desired behavior here at **THE CONSUMER UNDERGROUND.**

Living outside the box:

We will represent our best interests and not be taken advantage of. We will be confident, firm and fair while we represent our best interests. Utilizing this **confident objectivity**, we **facilitate the alignment** of companies' best interests with our expectations. We outline the **vision for the pathway to resolution** and **control the process** along the way. This results in a non-confrontational, stress free **win-win!**

CHAPTER 5

A POUND OF PREVENTION a.k.a. CONSUMER CONFLICT AVOIDANCE STRATEGIES:

It is better to light a candle than curse the darkness.

Eleanor Roosevelt

Illuminating strategies for navigating your way to an effective and stress-free consumer experience:

Bad Stuff Avoidance:

Don't shop somewhere where the checkout service is great, and the customer service/return area is a nightmare. If a company believes in their products, they will provide a reasonable return policy and demonstrate good product return service. The author will consider paying a premium for this level of service.

Here at **THE CONSUMER UNDERGROUND**, we choose to avoid the **"bad stuff"** by understanding that we are in control of minimizing negative outcomes. We avoid such negative outcomes by exercising critical thinking - what "bad stuff" will I encounter if I move in this direction? There is no consumer "escalator" providing positive direction to target our individual need - only the **herd**. But unlike the herd, free markets require **deliberate navigation**.

Some online stores are not actually affiliated with their brick and mortar namesake:

The author recently purchased a book online from a major brick and mortar national bookseller chain. Let's call this company "ACME books". The book that was ordered was unreadable due to the smallest print font known to exist on this earth. When attempting to return the unreadable book, the physical store refused to honor the return because they were **not affiliated** with the **online store** that shared their company namesake. Other retailers including some big box stores share this policy of not accepting returns of online purchases at their physical stores.

Lesson learned - **prior to purchasing** merchandise online from a brick and mortar retail chain, call the local physical store and ask if you can return any item that you purchase from them online. The time will come when you need to exercise the company's return policy. I keep that unreadable book as a reminder.

Review and understand; contracts, policies, warranties, loans, mortgages, deeds, etc. prior to commitment/signing:

The author is certainly no expert in this area and has only learned the importance of thoroughly reviewing and understanding important documents through the author's own failure to do so in the past. The reader would be well served to seek legal, financial, and other professional advice on this matter. The author can however share some lessons learned with the reader.

Recently, the author was preparing to sign what appeared to be a standard construction contract for a sizable residential renovation project. The construction contractor was a large company that was well known. Understanding the importance of thoroughly reviewing important documents prior to signing, a **troubling clause** was discovered near the end of the contract. The clause prohibited what is potentially the most effective point of leverage that a customer has. This clause essentially prohibited the contract signee from engaging in any derogatory **feedback via social media** if the project did not go well. Instead of focusing on earning positive reputational feedback by satisfying customers' needs, this contractor sought to "muzzle" the customers who were not satisfied with the performance of the contractor.

I chose not to do business with this contractor. Several months later, a friend informed me that their neighbor who hired this same contractor had a very unfavorable outcome on their construction project.

True Wisdom is Knowing What You Don't Know.

Confucius

Companies don't live forever:

A recent economic cycle in 2009 (which our government labeled "financial crisis") serves as a vivid reminder that **companies and institutions** don't live forever and will **ultimately fail.** It's just a matter of time - tomorrow or maybe a hundred, a thousand or ten thousand years – **no one knows.**

The author purchased tools that were warranted for life. They are **warranted** for life the **life of the Company,** and that company **expired** this year.

No company or institution is too big to fail. Take this into consideration when making a purchase decision. Also, I consider the following:

Who holds the warranty that you are considering purchasing - the company that manufactured (the general merchandise or automobile or computer or furnace or new house) or does a third-party service this warranty? If the third party holds the warranty will the manufacturer honor all warranty claims? What happens to the **warranty** when the **third-party** warranty company **goes out of business** or "reorganizes" or is bought out by another company or changes the original terms of the warranty?

Insurance.

The author certainly is not qualified to offer financial or insurance advice. Long term care insurance might indeed be perfect for your situation. We will look at long term care insurance simply as an exercise in critical thinking. The reader could substitute long term care insurance with almost any purchase decision opportunity in this exercise.

Let's look at long term care life insurance as a critical thinker. Are there any caps on increases to the periodic premiums or can the company **increase the premiums?** – let's say **100% per year as it pleases?** Let's say that you paid on this policy for 10 years. To keep the policy current, would you have to pay 20% more or even **double the amount** of the prior annual premium or face **losing all the $** that you contributed toward this policy? But Wait!...you paid the policy premium for ten years and the 100% annual increase last year, and the next year the company cannot fully fund this program or goes out of business. What happens to your $, your policy? These are examples of the questions that the critical thinker will explore prior to signing any contract and is the official mindset of **THE CONSUMER UNDERGROUND** - Pessimist? No. Optimistic Skeptic? Yes.

How long has the company been in business, what does their BBB profile look like?

Social media is becoming the standard for researching a company's history of performance. Here at **THE CONSUMER UNDERGROUND**, we encourage consumers to stay current with the fast evolving and expanding social media and digital platform spaces to fully utilize the value that these systems can provide. **Reputational feedback** and user reviews have become the standard performance measure for organizations. This feedback is a point of leverage for the consumer when the transaction does not meet expectations. The savvy consumer will research the organization's reputation and other feedback information prior to the purchase as a conflict avoidance strategy.

CHAPTER 6

THE DETAILED PROCESS

This section is for those times when we are not successful with the initial strategies outlined in the earlier chapters and we wish to pursue opportunities further to resolution. What follows is the **detailed - expanded** process on how to reach a remedy in these more challenging situations:

1)   **Is what you are seeking fair and reasonable?** Is the $ value **worth the time** and effort to pursue? Is this issue the responsibility of the company or **your fault?** See the section that follows these 8 steps for more discussion on fair and reasonable.

2)   **Identify point(s) of leverage** — the reason(s) why the company is **motivated** to **assist you** in reaching resolution. This is the most important step in the process and is rather simple to identify. You must identify **their interest** in settling **your issue**. Ask yourself if this is the person who has a **need** to resolve **your issue** - if so, this is leverage, if not you are wasting your time. Find this person. It might be the employee, supervisor, manager or owner who is **rated** on customer satisfaction criteria or complaint volume/social media feedback. Your favorable outcome may determine

their **bonus or advancement.** What about the honest or honorable employee, manager, or owner who wants to be fair to you? Company fear of negative public relations and company desire to maintain positive referral base of customers might be the is a prime motivation. Perhaps the company wants to maintain your repeat business, or the company made a mistake or miscalculation and wants to "make-it-right".

3)   **State your remedy** — you now become the advocate for this remedy. Determine your desired outcome. Make sure your desired outcome is fair and reasonable and communicate this desired outcome. Treat people like you would like to be treated - no one wants to help a rude, inconsiderate, pushy, threatening, demanding or condescending asshole! If you fit this description stop reading this book, this author does not want your $. Presume that you will reach your desired outcome/remedy. **Do not ask "if'** the company representative "can" provide your **desired outcome.** Ask rather if the representative "is the person" that will provide your desired outcome (e.g.; "are you the person that will exchange this air compressor for me, or is your supervisor?") stay calm and in control, if you are not calm, then they are in control - not you. **Confident objectivity** is the subtle yet powerful virtue that we are going to exude (this is the **secret sauce** in this process) - presume that you will succeed!

4)   **Use a hierarchical approach and don't lose sight of your point of leverage.** Start with the front-line supervisor and continue up the chain

of command as necessary. Presume that you will reach your desired outcome/remedy. Do not ask "if" the company representative "can" provide your desired outcome. Ask rather if the representative "is the person" that will provide your desired outcome. If you ask "if" the company "can" provide your desired remedy, you have given them the suggestion of denying what you are requesting. Don't waste time with someone who is not empathetic to your objective or who does not seem to be motivated to **advance your desired outcome**. When necessary move on to their boss and do not skip over any level of management or you will deny yourself the opportunity for all the middle managers/decision makers to remedy your request. Stay calm, courteous, direct, and polite throughout this process. Remain patient and focused on the **objective resolution**.

5)   **Restate the history of your dispute and your desired remedy at each stage of the company hierarchy.** You continue as the expediter and keep detailed notes of your discussion to accurately demonstrate the facts and therefore maintain your credibility and integrity.

6)   **After the company agrees to a mutual resolution, ask for a written confirmation of the remedy.** Send the representative a letter capturing the highlights of the phone conversation with your expectations. There are several examples of such letters in the Appendix. State the details of what the company promised and make sure such agreement includes a **date you will receive** the specified payment, merchandise, warranty, etc.

7)   **If the deadline has passed without the promised resolution, follow up on the issue.** Send a letter to restate your desired remedy and your expectations. See the sample letters in the Appendix for examples to use for this task. If the company fails to deliver on resolution that they communicated, go back to step #4.

8)   **Send letter of acknowledgement and gratitude to the boss of the person who delivered on the remedy.** Identify what you received and that your issue is resolved with the company. Send letter to the individual who helped resolve your issue and an **info copy to his/her boss.** See the sample letters in the Appendix as examples that you might use.

PROCESS TIPS:

Each level manager might only be able to offer you a **certain level of compensation.** Keep this in mind as you may be pursuing a remedy that the employee does not have the **authority** to grant in their **position.** When in doubt, ask this person if they have the authority to grant you your **remedy.** If they respond that they do not have such authority, ask them to please connect you with the person who does have such authority.

During your discussions with the supervisor/manager presume that they will help you. Give them a **good-faith opportunity** to grant your remedy.

By doing this, you set a positive dialogue. **Nice people want to help nice people**. It is human nature to avoid someone who is negative.

Remember to us the **hierarchical approach**. Do not **skip** from the front-line supervisor to the owner/CEO. If you jump up to the top of the chain of command, you will deny yourself the **opportunity** for all the middle managers and other decision makers to grant your remedy. Remember your **success** will be measured by the value of the remedy that you receive, not by how high you complain up the company chain of command. Relax, you can always reach the chief executive if needed, but if you execute this process effectively, you will reach a resolution much earlier (and quicker) with the front-line or middle managers.

Courage is the price that life exacts for granting peace.

Amelia Earhart

THE COURAGE TO BE CONFIDENT:

Confidence is **everything** in negotiating. If you doubt yourself, others will sense this and doubt you and you are less likely to be successful. Find confidence in yourself through this objective, proven process and focus on your point(s) of leverage before you pick up the phone or pen.

TIPS ON BUILDING CONFIDENCE FOR THIS PROCESS:

Be **honest** in assessing each consumer **opportunity** and believe in yourself and your objective plan first. Before you negotiate, review the steps of this process several times and even write out your answer to each step in the process. This is the time to second guess yourself - before you start the process - then **refine your strategy**. Feel confident about your answers to each step.

Now, do not look back and **doubt or second-guess** your plan. You have already come to terms with yourself on this matter (read the previous two sentences again). **You are now part of the plan**. This is your plan. You are representing something you believe in and you will know this and exude confidence and you will succeed. Move forward, pick up the phone confidently and successfully. You would lose your confidence if you allow yourself to second-guess your plan because you would be doubting yourself.

Save the **second-guessing** for **after** successfully resolving your issue and then use the process as a **lessons-learned critique**. We are not born with confidence. We find confidence from believing that we will succeed or from previous successes. Each time you succeed at this process, your confidence will come from the knowledge of your previous successes. You will rely more on past successes than the plan in this book for your future confidence. Now your strength becomes your confidence and **you become the plan**.

You will likely succeed if you follow this plan. Using this process, the author has successfully executed this so many times that the whole process becomes **reflexive**.

FAIR AND REASONABLE:

We must differentiate between a **legitimate concern** and a **poor purchase decision**, bad judgment, etc. It is always **our fault** as the consumer-customer when we fail to secure the most favorable terms for goods or services before we lay down the $. It is not an honorable option to negotiate these conditions after the unfavorable deal, which resulted from our lack of research, inattentiveness, failure to read the entire contract, etc. This is **our fault** and we can only try to learn from these mistakes.

(**THE BURN'S ON ME**) Recently, the author verbally agreed to pay a contractor twice as much as was reasonable much for a small job. I was in a hurry and was not paying attention but realized my mistake before this contractor had completed the job. Upon completion of the work, I paid him the agreed upon price, smiled, shook his hand, **thanked him for the fine work** as I ate the extra few hundred that I overpaid him — **my fault, my mistake**, my honor intact. I'll learn from this mistake - my mistake.

CHAPTER 7

THE CONSUMER CITIZEN - THE IMPACT OF GOVERNMENT POLICY AND TAXATION:

Loyalty to country always. Loyalty to government, when it deserves it.

Mark Twain

During a stint of government employment, the above quote hung at the entry to the author's government office. It was rarely well received by other government employees but was meant by the author as **inoculation** against **government hubris.**

Now let's go deeper into **THE CONSUMER UNDERGROUND.** We use critical thinking to ensure that our best interests are represented by "the governments". Along the way, we will solve **global pollution,** (which at the time of this writing, our governments refer to as **"climate change"**).

Governing - It's A Full Time Job!

The previous solution strategies explained in this book do not apply to any government or quasi-government entity. The reason is that the previous points of leverage do not motivate these governmental organizations to reach your desired outcome. But Wait!... yes indeed - the right to vote, the right to assemble.

To the government you are a citizen, not a customer/consumer. This is not a negative statement about any individuals that are employed by such organizations, certainly they employ many dedicated and effective workers.

As a **citizen**, you do not have the **leverage** available that you have as a **customer**. Governments are by nature, formed to govern over citizens and subjects, not to serve citizens' **wants**.

If the reader doubts the citizen's inability to leverage a desired outcome, the reader is invited to conduct a **field study** at the local **Department of Motor Vehicle Office**. Try negotiating reasonable wait times or reducing registration fees. The same applies to negotiating new terms of service, rates and expectations of service with; municipal trash removal, department of sewer and water, natural gas and electricity supplier, post office, IRS, Medicare, Medicaid, etc.

Trust Me...Trust Me Not:

Yet governments relentlessly attempt to **persuade citizens** that we need to hand over our remaining free market systems so that they can better manage such things. Can you imagine a **government run healthcare system** that resembles our local **D.M.V.** or post office?

Before we vote to expand the federal government's scope of managing anything in our lives, consider how the federal government has **grossly mismanaged** its own retirement system.

The federal government manages two retirement systems for its employees. The Federal Employees Retirement System (FERS) for employees hired after to 1986 and the Civil Service Retirement System (CSRS) for employees hired prior to 1986. The United States Federal Government currently employs about **2 million** workers. When employed, federal employees were required to make contributions into their respective retirement system.

But Wait!..the federal government (the employer) has not **contributed its portion** into either of the two retirement systems. As a result, there is an unfunded liability for retirees that is currently around **$800 billion!!!** There really is no retirement fund for federal workers or retirees. Federal workers and retirees are living on the **empty promise** of an **unfunded retirement!** Yet every city, county and state are required to maintain funds for their retirees. Some do better than others, but it is doubtful that there is a single government pension plan managed as dreadfully as the federal plans. Every private company that offers a pension plan (a.k.a. defined benefit plan) must follow **structured laws** and **rules** and fund their employees' pension plans.

How is the government performing on **social safety nets** - surely it can perform this most basic and necessary human need? Remember the Social Security **Trust Fund** that we contributed to? We were lied to. There is **no trust** and there is **no fund**. There is a **zero balance** in the Social Security Trust Fund. The Trust Fund was depleted and replaced with federal I.O.U.s - loans secured by treasury bonds - debt. This debt is what our federal government considers as assets in the Trust Fund. What happened is that the Congress has simply taken money collected for Social Security and Medicare, via payroll deductions and self-employment taxes, and used it for "other" purposes. That makes Social Security an unfunded liability. If you are retired or when you become a retiree, **you are an unfunded liability** to the government!

The narrative fallacy of political promise rings hollow on the ears of the critical thinker.

Pat Peterman

Rescuing Our Climate, The Easy Way:

Among numerous other ventures, the author has been in and out of the green-renewable-clean energy business since first working in solar power design in California in 1981.

Improving our climate's needs is shockingly **simple.** The government can incentivize photovoltaic solar panels for citizens to purchase and install on our residences. It's that easy viola - this is the solution. The End...But Wait...

For years, the amount of tax credits provided for residential solar panels has been **only a fraction** of what the comparable cost of using conventional (coal, gas, nuclear) electricity providers would be. Governments are very careful not to provide significant **incentives** that would provide motivation for **tens of millions** of citizens to install solar panels on our residences. If it did so, citizens would become **independent** of the government **controlled** and **taxed** electrical power grid. In fact, many governments **penalize** residential **solar** users to discourage it's use. Examples of some tactics used by governments to discourage/disincentivize residential solar power are; lack of realistic incentives, not allowing net zero metering, adding various "solar energy taxes" and constantly changing (reducing) electricity buy-back rates.

Where Did the Sun Go?

The lack of **adequate electrical energy storage** capacity is discussed as a reason that we need to just stick with the government controlled; coal, nuclear and natural gas power grid. But Wait! ...a **power storage solution** is already available. We could charge our electric vehicles from our residential rooftop solar panels instead of plugging them into the present electrical grid. Our **electric vehicle batteries** could be used to store energy for residential energy needs - lights, heat, etc. during the evening when no sun is available. The electric vehicle is in fact a **self-contained mobile energy storage solution!**

Presently most U. S. residences are powered by coal and natural gas burning electricity generating power plants. Residential solar systems that could recharge electric vehicles are not yet widely deployed. This means that currently, most **electric vehicles** in the U.S. are effectively **coal burners!**

Path to Independence – Tax Me...Tax Me Not!

As each residence possessed the means to produce, store, and use a free and **renewable** and **tax-free** energy source - photovoltaics, the energy

umbilical cord between citizens/subjects and the governments would be severed. How could governments tax or control such independence of its citizens? The government would be unable to tax our electricity or to tax the gas for our (electric) vehicles! Governments don't want a solution that creates such mass citizen independence and autonomy. This solution would also deny governments the massive tax revenue that it currently uses to control and manipulate citizen's behavior. Understand this relationship and it is obvious why we citizens are denied such independence.

How are all those government run urban mass transit strategies doing?

Government creates snake oil **tax strategies** like; gasoline taxes, electricity taxes, natural gas taxes, **water taxes, rain taxes, carbon taxes** and similar schemes. Governments keep us dependent on the electrical grid and the gasoline pump to generate taxes to fund **unrelated** under-funded government programs. Why do we consumer citizens fall for such **buffoonery**?

California Dreamin...California Schemin

Let's look at California's gasoline tax as an example. In 2019 Californians pay **65.7 cents** per gallon of gasoline **+ 9.75 percent** additional tax on top of the other tax! Even **electric car** owners are not shielded from the tax schemes as they are charged a **penalty fee** because they pay no tax at the gas pump! Many other states charge a **penalty tax on electric vehicles**.

These taxes were represented by government officials to taxpayers to; fund environmental cleanups, create incentives to reduce gasoline consumption, reduce smog, reduce carbon intensity of products, limit greenhouse gas emissions, fund road and bridge repairs, fund transportation improvement, provide a tax-swap. What voter would not wish to be a part of helping clean our environment, making roads safer and therefore support these important taxes? Perhaps some lawmakers had virtuous intentions when passing these taxes. But these taxes ended up **funding programs other than road projects and cleaning the environment.**

Where Did The $ Go?

Once again, the taxpayers were lied to under the guise of doing their fair-share for the environment. Does it make sense that a government that is so concerned with cleaning up the environment would impose a **penalty tax** on **electric vehicles?** Sadly, in California not hundreds of millions - but over a **BILLION dollars** have been raided from the **trust fund** that was created from the gasoline sales taxes and the penalty tax for owning electric vehicles. The money that was raided from the transportation trust fund was diverted from fixing bridges and filling potholes and cleaning the environment and was spent on other purposes.

How does this help curtail "climate change" and improve "road safety"? This is just one example of a government tax that is actually a convenient and nontransparent way of raising more revenue to feed a **chronic government overspending** habit. Remember this example as your government continues to extol the virtues of any new tax such as a "carbon tax" on its **citizenry/serfs**.

More Tomfoolery:

At the time of this writing, the federal government is at it again with yet another **new proposed gasoline tax**. Of course, consumers are most vulnerable to accepting such tax increases when fuel prices are low.

New **dubious tax** proposals to satisfy **nebulous needs**! These **lawmakers** must be **laughing** at taxpayers who pay them to toast each other and lavishly dine in the comfort and safety of their high walled **mansions** surrounded by **armed security details** (armed with "assault weapons" of course)!

The critical thinkers here at **THE CONSUMER UNDERGROUND** don't fall for these **shenanigans**.

The Power of Knowledge – The Responsibility of Action:

You now have insight to "little known secrets to save consumers thousands of $ per year." I wish you successful outcomes in deploying the strategies outlined in this book. Even a **single** such outcome will have made the study **worthwhile**. If you **seriously embrace** the strategies and **immerse** yourself into critical thinking, it could **change your life**.

Be mindful of the potential negative outcomes in using the strategies in this book. **Avoid engaging in the action of defamation**! You could be sued and loose everything. There is no substitute for competent professional advice for; legal, financial, insurance, real estate, investing, contracts, etc. The author makes no claims as an authority on such matters. This book does not represent advise or expertise on any of those subjects.

Please browse the Appendix. The author developed the sample letters in the **Appendix** to save the reader the time of drafting them. All letters in the **Appendix** are examples used in **real life** successful solution strategies by the author.

It was the author's intent through the gratuitous use of wry wit, the reader would be offered the occasion to crack a **smile**. If you engaged this episodic amusement during the reading of this book, feel free to **share** that **smile** with **everyone** you meet. **CHEERS**!

Appendix A

Use this e-mail sample for written confirmation of insurance representative claim visit re-weather/hail.

From: Pat Peterman

To: ACME Insurance Inc.

Dear: Mr. Roger Remedy,

Thank you for meeting me at my home yesterday, May 12, 2019 to inspect the damage of my property.

During the inspection, I presented you with photographs that were taken during the hail event. I also provided you with archived weather data specific to location and date. This included satellite imagery which pinpointed a severe weather event at the location of my property.

You indicated that my roof was a total loss and the gutters would need to be replaced and painted with two coats of paint. You documented that the window sills and house siding would need to be painted as a result of the hail impacting these areas.

During a survey of the back and front yard, you documented the damage to the fencing that would need to be re-stained. Also documented were; the patio table and chairs, flower pots and deck finish, which you stated would all need to be repaired or replaced.

Thank you for your thorough on-site claim review and open communication during this process. It is reassuring to know that all the property that was damaged during the severe weather event will be repaired or replaced by your company, as my insurer for such losses.

I look forward to putting the memory of the storm behind me and having my home back like it was before the storm. The $38,000.00 settlement check that your company agreed to for reimbursement for the above outlined property damage is necessary to facilitate this process.

Will this check by mailed to me by May 21, 2019 as previously promised?
Sincerely,

Pat Peterman

12345 Main St.

Nowhere, NW 12345

Appendix B

REAL WORLD EXAMPLES of CONSUMER STRATEGIES #2

e-mail sample-written pursuit of remedy re-automobile recurring reliability issues

From: Pat Peterman

To: ACME Automobile Inc.

Ms. Wendy Wheeler, Consumer Affairs

Dear: Ms. Wheeler,

Thank you for our phone discussion yesterday, November 14, 2019.

During our discussion yesterday, you stated that you agreed with me that my two years old ACME Silver Express Minivan has experienced more electronic control failures than is considered normal. You advised me to send you a letter outlining the negative impact that those electric failures have had on me and my family.

Since I purchased my ACME Silver Express Minivan last May, I have experienced four failures of electrical control systems.

The first electrical failure was on June 9, 2018. I was without the vehicle for 3 days and had to take time off from work to bring the vehicle in for service and pick it up after the service was completed.

The second electrical failure was on September 21, 2018. I was without the vehicle for 5 days and had to take time off from work to bring the vehicle in for service and pick it up after the service was completed. I paid out of pocket $342.00 for a rental car for this timeframe.

The third electrical failure was on October 14, 2019. I was without the vehicle for 2 days and had to take time off from work to take the vehicle in for service and pick it up after the service was completed.

The fourth electrical failure was on November 9, 2019. I was without the vehicle for 3 days and had to take time off from work to take the vehicle in for service and pick it up after the service was completed.

The service advisor did not seem that confident that they have the recurring electrical failure figured out. This is an ongoing problem and I have little confidence in the reliability of my ACME Silver Express Minivan.

Because of the above mechanical failures, I have had to take off many hours off from my work that I will not be reimbursed for. Many hours were also spent communicating with the service advisor to coordinate the repairs and scheduling of the automobile transportation to and from the dealership service center.

I understand that these issues have been repaired as covered by my warranty. This is not the issue.

Last May, when I purchased the new ACME Silver Express Minivan for $42,460.00. I was excited to experience the reliability and luxury of a brand-new car. Unfortunately, the promise of excellence of ACME Automobile Inc. has not been reality for me and my family.

In consideration of the above facts, you agreed that ACME Automobile Inc. company will act with integrity by remedying my situation and offer me consideration for the inconveniences and lost time at my work that I incurred. You mentioned that in situations such as mine, that it is often appropriate that ACME compensates me for my next month car payment ($685.00) and reimbursement for the $342.00 car rental. I have enclosed a receipt of the $342.00 car rental with ACME Rentals.

I am enclosing my car loan information per your request:

Loan # 1234567

My Bank's Routing # 1234567

My Bank's Account # 1234567

Thank you for providing me with assurances that your company will earn back my trust in the ACME brand by remedying my situation as I have described in this correspondence. Please feel free to contact me with any questions. I look forward to receiving a response from you as promised by November 24, 2019.

Sincerely,

Pat Peterman

12345 Main St.

Nowhere, NW 12345

Appendix C

REAL WORLD EXAMPLES of CONSUMER STRATEGIES #3

e-mail sample-request for remedy to internet retailer

From: Pat Peterman

To: (retrieve the seller's previous e-mail that you received when you purchased the item and reply to their e-mail)

Subject: (enter the seller's item # and order # here followed by re- your last name)

Dear: Ms. Illumination,

I was excited to purchase and receive my solar powered outside lights #xxxx that I ordered from you on xxxx. Based on the numerous positive reviews of these lights, your company's upstanding reputation, and after reading your product description, I was sure that these lights would be a perfect solution for my outside porch lighting needs.

After I first installed the lights, I was impressed with the amount of light and how long the batteries held a charge -just like in the reviews! Unfortunately, after a few months, the lights stopped working. I am disappointed that the lights failed to work as represented and am contacting you about replacing them with units that work as advertised.

I look forward to receiving the replacement units so that I can enjoy the same positive experience as thousands of your other customers. I look forward to providing prompt positive feedback regarding this issue.

Sincerely,

Pat Peterman

12345 Main St.

Nowhere, NW 12345

Appendix D

REAL WORLD EXAMPLES of CONSUMER STRATEGIES #4

Use this to request replacement, refund or store credit for merchandise that failed to meet your expectations after warranty period expired. You previously attempted to return item to store where you purchased the item with no success. (Such as in Solution Strategy #4)

Conduct an internet search for the vacuum cleaner manufacturer and make a few calls to find the contact that can assist you. I usually follow the detailed process in chapter 6 with this contact prior to sending any correspondence. Or, if you prefer, you can send a letter without talking to this contact. Our points of leverage here are that the vacuum was defective prior to the expiration of the warranty period and the vacuum is a safety/fire hazard. This letter is an example of how I would respond to a company that is initially reluctant to grant a desired remedy.

From: Pat Peterman

To: ACME Vacuum Inc.

Subject: ACME Platinum Plus Vacuum Cleaner

Dear: Mr. Stanley Stringent,

On February 3, 2019, I purchased an ACME Platinum Plus Vacuum Cleaner Model# Serial# from Big Box Inc. for $500.00. The decision to purchase this vacuum was made with consideration of your company's longstanding reputation of excellence in manufacturing vacuum cleaners. This is the third vacuum that I have purchased from ACME and have been a loyal customer for over 15 years.

The vacuum cleaner seemed to work as advertised during the 90-day warranty period, but I do remember an electrical burning smell during that time. After that time, the motor started smoking more and making odd electrical sounds like it was short-circuiting. Also, the vacuum cleaner started tripping my circuit breakers in our main electrical panel.

I talked with an electrician friend who told me that this seems like an electrical hazard and fire hazard. Because of this, I stopped using my ACME Platinum Plus vacuum cleaner.

I understand that the 90-day warranty period has expired, but the burning smell present during the warranty period was obviously not normal and was an indication that the unit was defective.

Even though the vacuum had only a 90-day limited warranty, it is fair and reasonable for a long-time, loyal customer to have expectations of excellence from your company and your brand. At a minimum, your product should not introduce an electrical and fire hazard into my home!

In consideration of the above facts, it is fair and reasonable to request that ACME replace my ACME Platinum Plus vacuum cleaner with a unit that is safe! Thank you in advance for replacing my unsafe vacuum cleaner.

Sincerely,

Pat Peterman

12345 Main St.

Nowhere, NW 12345

Appendix E

REAL WORLD EXAMPLES of CONSUMER STRATEGIES #6

e-mail sample — written pursuit of remedy to automobile manufacturer re-automobile reliability issues

From: Pat Peterman

To: ACME Automotive Inc.

Dear: Mr. Harry Hubkap:

Thank you for our phone discussion yesterday, May 2, 2019. You requested that I provide a detailed timeline and narrative outlining the problems that I have had with my 2019 ACME 4x4 Triplecab truck. This letter serves to satisfy that request.

I purchased my 2016 ACME 4x4 Triplecab truck in February of 2016 and I have had all service performed at ACME Automotive Big Johnson's Dealership. I have purchased new ACME vehicles in the past and have recommended them to my family and friends (both my sister and parents recently purchased new ACME trucks-my mother's second in two years). I have had great experience with ACME trucks and subsequently have developed high expectations for their reliability.

On April 5, 2019, at only 24,408 miles, my ACME 4x4 Triplecab was repaired for an air conditioning manifold leak, which resulted in total charges of $1,193.43. It took a second trip to ACME Automotive Big Johnson's Dealership (and another five-mile bike ride from home) to have it re-fixed (during the first repair, the equipment at Big Johnson's overcharged the a/c system).

On April 15, at only 25,221 miles, my ACME Triplecab was repaired for a transmission replacement. After discussions with ACME Automotive Customer Service Division, (and after initially being told repeatedly that there was nothing that they could do for me), I ended up paying $4,280.00 to have the transmission with only 25,221 miles replaced with a new one.

My expectations for the ACME 4x4 Triplecab truck were that I would realize more than 24,408 miles of air conditioning utility prior to the failure of this system. My expectations were that I would realize more than 25,221 miles of transmission utility prior to the total failure of the transmission. Of course, these failures happened only 2 months after the expiration of my new vehicle's 3-year, 40,000 miles warranty.

I would like to believe my experience is the exception. I trust that you will preserve the credibility and integrity of ACME Automotive Inc. and stand behind the unfortunate mechanical and service failures that I have experienced. To accomplish this, I believe it fair for ACME Automotive to reimburse me for the above expenses. I feel that my expectations for reliability have been reasonable. I would like to once again purchase and recommend your products.

If you feel however, that my expectations for reliability for my 2016 ACME 4x4 Triplecab truck have been unreasonable, and that the above failures should be expected from ACME products - just two months out of the warranty period, with much less mileage than allotted during the warranty period. Please forward the name, address and phone number of the ACME Vice President of Customer relations so that I may discuss this matter with him/her.

Please reply to this letter by May 14, 2019. Thank you in advance for standing behind your product and service network.

Sincerely,

Pat Peterman

12345 Main St.

Nowhere, NW 12345

Appendix F

REAL WORLD EXAMPLES of CONSUMER STRATEGIES

e-mail sample — written pursuit of remedy to automobile manufacturer - use this e-mail to pursue consideration for automobile that you purchased new and have had too many reliability repairs (under warranty)

From: Pat Peterman

To: ACME Automobile Inc.

Mr. Matt Motorman, Consumer Affairs

Dear: Mr. Motorman,

Thank you for our phone discussion yesterday, October 21, 2019.

During our discussion yesterday, you stated that you agreed with me that my one-year old ACME Triple Platinum Deluxe Sedan has experienced many more mechanical failures than is considered normal. You advised me to send you a letter outlining the negative impact that those mechanical failures have had on me and my family.

Since I purchased my ACME Triple Platinum Deluxe Sedan last May, I have experienced seven mechanical failures of various engine, electrical and transmission systems. One of these failures have resulted in me being stranded in the vehicle and needing to be towed into local ACME Automobile dealerships for repair.

The first mechanical failure was a water pump on May 5, 2019. I was without the vehicle for 5 days and had to take time off from work take the vehicle in for service and pick it up after the service was completed.

The second mechanical failure was a transmission sensor on June 4, 2019. I was without the vehicle for 3 days and had to take time off from work time to take the vehicle in for service and pick it up after the service was completed.

The third mechanical failure was an electrical sensor failure on August 17, 2019. I was without the vehicle for 2 days and had to take time off from work to take the vehicle in for service and pick it up after the service was completed.

The fourth mechanical failure was an engine management system failure on August 28, 2019. This failure resulted in me being stranded in the vehicle and needing to be towed. 1 WAS STRANDED ON THE SIDE OF HIGHWAY IN DANGEROUS TRAFFIC FOR 2 HOURS!! I was without the vehicle for 6 days and had to take time off from work to take the vehicle in for service and pick it up after the service was completed.

The fifth mechanical failure was on September 9, 2019. I was without the vehicle for I day due to another electric engine management system failure and had to take time off from work to take the vehicle in for service and pick it up after the service was completed. This is a recurring problem on the car and the one that caused me to be stranded with my two dogs on the side of the highway on August 28, 2019.

The sixth mechanical failure was on September 20, 2019. I was without the vehicle for 1 day due to another electric engine management system failure and had to take time off from work to take the vehicle in for service and pick it up after the service was completed. The service advisor did not seem that confident that they have the engine management system failure figured out.

The seventh mechanical failure was on October 17, 2019. I was without the vehicle for 2 days due to another electric engine management system failure and had to take time off from work to take the vehicle in for service and pick it up after the service was completed. The service advisor did not seem that confident that they have the engine management system failure figured out.

Because of the above mechanical failures, I have had to take off many hours off from my work that I will not be reimbursed for. Many hours were also spent communicating with the service advisor to coordinate the repairs and scheduling of the automobile transportation to and from the dealership service center. I understand that these issues have been repaired as covered by my warranty and that a rental car was provided during the service periods. This is not the issue.

Last May, when I purchased the new red Triple Platinum Deluxe Sedan for $39,540.00. I was excited to experience the reliability and luxury of a new car. Unfortunately, the promise of excellence that ACME Automobile Inc. has not been reality for me and my family. In consideration of the above facts, you agreed that ACME Automobile Inc. will offer me consideration for the inconveniences and lost time at my work that I incurred. You mentioned that in a few situations such as mine, a manufacturer's extended warranty (bumper-to-bumper) was grated to other owners. You stated that an extended warranty would be considered to offer me peace-of-mind for any possible long-term maintenance issues.

Thank you for providing me with assurances that your company will act will integrity by remedying my situation as I have described in this correspondence. Please feel free to contact me with any questions. I look forward to receiving a response from you as promised by October 28, 2019.

Sincerely,

Pat Peterman

12345 Main St.

Nowhere, NW 12345

Appendix G

REAL WORLD EXAMPLES of CONSUMER STRATEGIES

e-mail sample written confirmation of remedy -use this e-mail to confirm discussion of resolution to remind company of the terms that they promised, and include a date when they committed to deliver on such promise to you, this e-mail serves to document the discussion and promised remedy, reminds them of their commitment, and becomes a useful document (point of leverage) if the company fails to deliver on the promise

From: Pat Peterman

To: ACME recliner stores Inc.

Dear: Ms. Loungir,

Thank you for our phone discussion yesterday, May 12, 2019.

During our discussion, you stated that you understood that the reclining chair that I purchased last November for $1,110.00 was defective. The reclining mechanism has been intermittently failing to engage for months, and some fabric is separating at the seams near the armrest.

You also stated that even though this reclining chair carried only a 30-day limited warranty, that it is fair and reasonable for a customer to have expectations of excellence from your company and your brand. Also, you agreed that those reasonable quality expectations have not been met in my situation as loyal customer.

In consideration of the above facts, you agreed to accept the return of the defective reclining chair for full refund of the original $1,110.00.

I understand that the store where I purchase the reclining chair will pick up the chair from my residence on May 21, between 3:00pm and 5:00pm. I further understand that I will receive a company check in the mail by May 25, 2019.

During our discussion, you also stated that I would receive a letter from your claim's management department stating what I am summarizing in this letter. You stated that I would receive that correspondence by May 14, 2019.

Thank you for providing me with assurances that your company will remedy my situation as I have described in this correspondence.

Sincerely,

Pat Peterman

12345 Main St.

Nowhere, NW 12345

Appendix H

REAL WORLD EXAMPLES of CONSUMER STRATEGIES

e-mail sample - request to internet retailer for replacement for merchandise that failed to work after (30 day) warranty period expired - this is your first communication with this company

From: Pat Peterman

To: (retrieve the seller's previous e-mail that you received when you purchased the item and reply to their e-mail)

Subject: (enter the seller's item # and order # here followed by re- your last name)

Dear: Mr. Shortbreeze,

Based on the numerous positive reviews of these fans, your company's upstanding reputation, and after reading your product description, I was sure that the fan model would be a great at cooling my kitchen.

When I first used the fan, it worked great and was extremely quiet - just like in the reviews! Unfortunately, after a few months, the fan started making a very loud noise and started turning much slower than when new. Now, it does not even rotate when turned on!

I am disappointed that the fan failed to work as represented and am contacting you about replacing the fan with one that lasts longer than a few months. For $235.00, this fan failed to meet the value that your company represented.

I look forward to receiving a replacement unit for this premium priced product so that I can enjoy the same positive experience as thousands of your other customers. I look forward to providing prompt positive feedback regarding this issue after I receive the replacement fan.

Sincerely,

Pat Peterman

12345 Main St.

Nowhere, NW 12345

Appendix I

REAL WORLD EXAMPLES of CONSUMER STRATEGIES

use this e-mail for follow-up after no success talking with several managers in this company - the issue in this sample letter is for poor repair service on a product.

From: Pat Peterman

To: ACME Furnace Inc.

Dear: Ms. Alotta Hottaire:

Thank you for our phone discussion yesterday, February 27, 2020.

When researching the BBB, and internet and social media sites for furnace repair companies, I found that your company had very high customer satisfaction. I made the decision to use your company for my furnace repair needs based on these positive reviews.

On January 5, your company conducted cleaning and a "safety inspection" of the furnace. Your technician, Rob, recommended replacing the blower motor on my furnace for preventative maintenance and safety due to possible carbon monoxide issues if the fan ran at low performance. The service charge to clean, inspect, and replace this motor was $1,230.00.

On January 9, the furnace blower stopped working. On January 10, your company replaced the furnace blower servo control for $367.00.

On February 19, the furnace blower stopped working again. On February 20, your company replaced the blower motor and blower motor servo (again). On February 22, I received a bill of $982.00 for this service.

On February 22, I contacted Brian, the scheduling supervisor to discuss the blower and servo having been replaced just over a month prior to the February 20 visit. Brian informed me that the replaced parts carry a warranty of only 30 days. Brian stated that the warranty was company policy and that there was nothing that he could to about it.

On February 22 - February 26, I called 21 times and left messages to talk to the general manager or owner of the company. My calls were not returned.

Finally, on February 27, I was able to contact you. I appreciate that you (as area sales manager) are willing to represent my situation to the owner of the company.

When we talked yesterday, you stated that you understood my concerns that during an annual furnace inspection, your company representative recommended replacing a functioning furnace blower motor. The replacement motor failed after just over 30 days of use - only several days out of warranty!

The replaced blower motor servo also failed after only 37 days of use - just 7 days past warranty!

You also agreed that it was not acceptable for you company management to not return my 21 phone calls over 5 days!

You stated that you agreed with me that my recent overall experience with ACME Furnace did not meet with the promise of excellence that your company represents.

I stated that a fair and reasonable remedy in this situation would be to waive the $982.00 for the February 20 service that was to replace parts that your company had installed just the month prior. You stated that this remedy made sense and that you would represent this remedy to the owner of the company when he returns from The Bahamas and Aruba tomorrow.

Thank you for providing me with assurances that your company will remedy my situation as I have described in this correspondence. I look forward to your response on March 4, 2020 as you committed.

Sincerely,

Pat Peterman

12345 Main St.

Nowhere, NW 12345

Appendix J

REAL WORLD EXAMPLES of CONSUMER STRATEGIES

e-mail sample — remedy has passed without the promised resolution - use this e-mail to confirm discussion of resolution and remind company of the terms that they promised and that the date they promised such remedy has passed - we use an exception of the hierarchical approach in this case because a company representative failed to deliver on a resolution that they committed to in writing

From: Pat Peterman

To: ACME recliner stores Inc.

Dear: Ms. Loungir,

We first talked on the phone, May 12, 2019.

During that discussion, you stated that you understood that the reclining chair that I purchased last November for $1,110.00 was defective. The reclining mechanism has been intermittently failing to engage for months, and some fabric is separating at the seams near the armrest.

You also stated that even though this reclining chair carried only a 30 day limited warranty, that it is fair and reasonable for a customer to have expectations of excellence from your company and your brand, Also, you agreed that those reasonable quality expectations have not been met in my situation as loyal customer.

In consideration of the above facts, you also agreed to accept the return of the defective reclining chair for full refund of the original $1,110.00.

I understood that the store where I purchase the reclining chair was to pick up the chair from my residence on May 21, between 3:00pm and 5:00pm. I further understood that I would receive a company check in the mail by May 25, 2019.

During our discussion, you also stated that I would receive a letter from your claims' management department stating what I am summarizing in this letter. You stated that I would receive that correspondence by May 14, 2019. I did receive this correspondence.

You provided me with assurances that your company would remedy my situation as I described in the previous correspondence dated May 12, 2019.

It is now May 28, 2019 and the defective recliner was picked up from my home on May 21, 2019 as agreed to. However, I have not yet received your company's refund check for $1,110.00 as promised.

Ms. Loungir, your company is now in possession of the reclining chair that I purchased from your company on November 7, 2019. I have performed all obligations that we agreed to in the May 14 letter of commitment that I received from you. In that letter, you committed to issue a check for $1,110.00 to me by May 25, 2019. You have failed to deliver on that promise. Please provide me with your company owner's name, title, address and phone number so that I can hold your company accountable for your commitment.

Sincerely,

Pat Peterman

12345 Main St.

Nowhere, NW 12345

Appendix K

REAL WORLD EXAMPLES of CONSUMER STRATEGIES

e-mail sample - use this e-mail to confirm discussion of resolution and remind company of the terms that they promised and that the date they promised such remedy has passed - this company sent us an E-mail agreeing to replace the defective product - we use an exception of the hierarchical approach in this case because a company representative failed to deliver on a resolution that they committed to in writing

From: Pat Peterman

To: ACME Food Processors Inc.

Subject: (enter the seller's item # and order # here followed by re- your last name)

Dear: Mr. Mitch Mixitup,

I was looking forward to receiving my Bronze Edition Super Food Processor with 13 removable attachments #xxxx that I ordered from you on xxxx. I read many of the glowing reviews about the processor. I based my purchase of the food processor on your company's upstanding reputation. I was looking forward to the effortless food preparation as depicted in your video advertisements. I decided that the processor with attachments must be worth the $562.00 asking price.

For 4 months, I was amazed at the ease of food preparations using all the different attachments - just like in the reviews and videos! Unfortunately, after a few months, the Bronze Edition Super Food Processor stopped working.

I was disappointed that the food processor failed to work as represented, I contacted you on June 3, 2019 about replacing them with units that work as advertised even though the processor was several months past your company warranty period. You agreed that I should be sent a replacement processor so that I could enjoy the same positive experience as thousands of your other customers. On June 9, 2019, I received your reply that you committed to replacing my Bronze Edition Super Food Processor with a brand new one that I would receive by June 27, 2019.

Unfortunately, it is now July 7, 2019 and I have yet to receive my new food processor as promised. This failure certainly does not meet the expectation of excellence that your company advertises.

You have failed to deliver on your written commitment to replace my $562.00 Bronze Edition Super Food Processor with 13 removable attachments by June 27, 2019. Please provide me with your company owner's name, title, address and phone number so that I can hold you accountable for your promised remedy.

Sincerely,

Pat Peterman

12345 Main St.

Nowhere, NW 12345

Appendix L

REAL WORLD EXAMPLES of CONSUMER STRATEGIES

e-mail sample — written thank you letter - use this e-mail to identify what you received and that your issue is resolved with the company - make sure to c.c. the boss(s) of person who assisted you in resolving your issue - start the letter with a summary of the issue - a short history (good for future reference if needed)

From: Pat Peterman

To: ACME recliner stores Inc.

Dear: Ms. Loungir,

Thank you, Ms. Loungir for your assistance with the resolution of the below warranty/quality issue:

You agreed that you understood that the reclining chair that I purchased last November for $1,110.00 was defective. The reclining mechanism has been intermittently failing to engage for months, and some fabric is separating at the seams near the armrest.

You also stated that even though this reclining chair carried only a 30 days limited warranty, it is fair and reasonable for a customer to have expectations of excellence from your company and your brand. Also, you agreed that those reasonable quality expectations have not been met in my situation as a loyal customer.

In consideration of the above facts you agreed to accept the return of the defective reclining chair for full refund of the original $ 1,110.00.

The store where I purchase the reclining chair picked up the chair from my residence on May 21. I received a company check in the mail on May 24, 2019 for the full refund of $1,110.00.

Again, Ms. Loungir, thank you for helping me resolve this issue and therefore fulfilling the promise of excellence that I expected from ACME.

Sincerely,

Pat Peterman

12345 Main St.

Nowhere, NW 12345

Appendix M

REAL WORLD EXAMPLES of CONSUMER STRATEGIES

e-mail sample - use to send to the insurance representative to inform them of the car manufacturer's position on auto glass replacement - include the manufacture's important recommendation for OEM glass replacement due to numerous safety considerations - the automobile manufacture's recommendation based on safety reasons is our point of leverage that will be the cornerstone of this e-mail

From: Pat Peterman

To: ACME Insurance Company Inc.

Dear: Mr. Bin Triento-Cheatum,

Thank you for our phone discussion yesterday regarding the replacement of the cracked windshield on my 2018 ACME Hybrid Greenaire Sedan. My policy # is xxxxxxxxx.

When we talked on the phone yesterday, you stated that my policy for comprehensive automobile coverage does not cover the replacement of my damaged windshield with a windshield that is Original Equipment Manufacturer (OEM) provided. You stated that ACME Insurance partners with an auto glass replacement company that provides a replacement automobile glass which meets all the requirements of the United States

Department of Transportation (DOT). You also stated that there would be a cost to me of $940.00 to upgrade to the OEM windshield replacement. This cost is in addition to my $500.00 deductible for comprehensive coverage.

After our discussion, I searched ACME Automotive website and found the following safety information regarding replacing any glass on my 2018 ACME Hybrid Greenaire Sedan:

"ACME Automotive Advanced Driver Assistance Systems such as: adaptive cruise control, glare-free high beam, pixel light, adaptive light control, automatic parking, collision mitigation braking system, blind spot monitor, automatic night vision, navigation system, forward collision warning, radar, camera, lane departure warning, advanced driver assistance system, etc. all require ocular clarity and accuracy. The windshields on all ACME vehicles are specifically designed and manufactured to extreme quality tolerances to integrate with these advanced vehicle technologies. Aftermarket glass does not always account for these complex electrical component arrays and may interfere with ACME Automotive electronic safety systems or cause them to not function properly. This could create an unsafe condition for the occupants of the vehicle. Also, some glass components on ACME vehicles, especially the windshield, are engineered and manufactured as integrated structural components necessary for successful safety performance during a potential collision or rollover event. Due to these numerous safety considerations, it is ACME Automotive position that we recommend OEM glass for any glass replacement on all ACME vehicles."

Mr. Triento-Cheatum, ACME Automotive recommends OEM glass for any glass replacement on all ACME vehicles due to numerous safety requirements. ACME Automotive states that such recommendation for OEM glass replacement is to ensure the safety of my 2018 ACME Hybrid Greenaire Sedan. Based on my car manufacturer's safety recommendation, I do not believe that it is reasonable for ACME Insurance Company to pressure me to replace my damaged windshield with an unsafe aftermarket windshield. I should not be required to pay the additional cost of $940.00 to return my vehicle to the safe condition that it was in prior to the windshield becoming damaged.

I do not feel safe driving myself and my family in a vehicle that does not provide the equivalent level of safety that my car had when new. Please provide me with the safe OEM windshield replacement for my 2018 ACME Hybrid Greenaire Sedan at no additional cost to me. Please process this request today, as I need to expedite the repair of my 2018 ACME Hybrid Greenaire Sedan back into a safe condition so that I can use it on my daily commute to work.

If ACME Insurance Company refuses to replace my car's windshield with safe OEM glass (as ACME Automotive recommended for various safety considerations) at no additional cost to me, please provide this denial for OEM glass replacement in writing to me.

Sincerely,

Pat Peterman

12345 Main St.

Nowhere, NW 12345

About the Author

Petroleum Refining Operations

Automobile Rental services

Automobile Sales

Logger

U.S. Marine Corps

Emergency Medical Technician

Residential and Commercial Solar Design

U. S. Army

Accident Investigation

Forensic Engineering

Business Systems Sales

Communications Engineering

Operations Management

Logistics Management

Training Management

Real Estate Sales Management

Information Systems Management

Configuration Control Management

Project Integration Management

National Research Laboratory Construction Management

National Research Laboratory Risk Management

National Research Laboratory Quality Management

www.ingramcontent.com/pod-product-compliance
Lightning Source LLC
Chambersburg PA
CBHW022018170526
45157CB00003B/1275